New Frontiers of Space

Cutting-Edge

Space Tourism

Kevin Kurtz

Lerner Publications ◆ Minneapolis

Lerner Publications Company
An imprint of Lerner Publishing Group, Inc.
241 First Avenue North
Minneapolis, MN 55401 USA

For reading levels and more information, look up this title at www.lernerbooks.com.

Main body text set in Adrianna Regular 14/20.
Typeface provided by Chank.

Library of Congress Cataloging-in-Publication Data

Names: Kurtz, Kevin, author.
Title: Cutting-edge space tourism / Kevin Kurtz.
Other titles: Cutting edge space tourism
Description: Minneapolis: Lerner Publications, [2019] | Series: Searchlight books. New frontiers of space | Audience: Ages 8–11. | Audience: Grades 4 to 6.
Identifiers: LCCN 2018057822 (print) | LCCN 2019002403 (ebook) | ISBN 9781541557475 (eb pdf) | ISBN 9781541557444 (lb : alk. paper) | ISBN 9781541574861 (pb : alk. paper)
Subjects: LCSH: Space tourism—Juvenile literature. | Manned space flight—Juvenile literature. | Interplanetary voyages—Juvenile literature. | Outer space—Civilian use—Juvenile literature.
Classification: LCC TL794.7 (ebook) | LCC TL794.7 .K87 2019 (print) | DDC 910.919—dc23

LC record available at https://lccn.loc.gov/2018057822

Manufactured in the United States of America
1-46153-45952-5/6/2019

Contents

Chapter 1

TOURISTS IN SPACE

On April 28, 2001, the Russian *Soyuz TM-32* spacecraft fired its rockets. It lifted off the ground and headed toward space. Looking out the spacecraft's window was an unusual passenger. He was not an astronaut. He was US businessman and engineer Dennis Tito. That day, Tito accomplished one of his biggest dreams. He became the world's very first space tourist.

From left to right: Crew members Dennis Tito, Talgat Musabayev, and Yuri Baturin wave from inside the space station.

A VIEW FROM INSIDE THE INTERNATIONAL SPACE STATION (ISS)

Tito had paid $20 million for his ticket to space. This expensive price bought him nearly eight days in space. After two days orbiting Earth, Tito arrived at the ISS. He stared out of the windows at the incredible view. He saw the blackness of space and Earth curving below him while he listened to opera music. Tito returned home after six days on the station. Being a space tourist changed his life. What he saw in space stayed with him forever.

Government Space Travel

The first spaceships were not built for tourists. Different countries built them to carry astronauts, satellites, and science equipment into space. The people aboard all worked for governments.

The National Aeronautics and Space Administration (NASA) is the US government's space agency.

The first space tourists launched using Russian rockets, such as the Soyuz.

Spaceships are very expensive to launch. Many of them can be used only once. It costs hundreds of millions of dollars to build new ships and rockets for each trip. And space is limited inside the ships. Until 2001, only astronauts went into space to do scientific research.

Tito was the first tourist. Since him, six more tourists have visited space. Each person paid millions of dollars for the experience.

Very few people get to work as astronauts. And not many people have millions of dollars to spend on a ticket. But some companies want to make it easier to go to space. They are building the first spaceships intended just for tourists. The companies hope to make space travel cheaper. Then more people will be able to afford a ticket to travel into space. Maybe you could be a space tourist someday!

Blue Origin is one company that is building spaceships and rockets for space tourism.

Where Does Space Begin?

Space is not so far away. Most scientists agree that it begins about 62 miles (100 km) above sea level. Scientists call this the Karman line. Above this boundary there is not enough air for planes to fly. A tourist needs to travel past this line to be in space.

Space begins at the edge of Earth's atmosphere.

Chapter 2

BUILDING A BETTER SPACESHIP

Different companies are racing to build spaceships for tourists. Virgin Galactic, SpaceX, and Blue Origin are a few examples. These companies are designing shuttles, capsules, and rockets. Many of them can be reused. Reusing spaceships makes them cheaper to fly. That helps make passenger tickets cheaper too.

Blue Origin's New Shepard spacecraft is being tested for human flight.

Fins on a SpaceX rocket help it land back on Earth after takeoff.

These companies have designed rockets that can land, instead of just crashing back to Earth. Metal fins on the rocket help its engine point down as it falls. When the rocket is almost to the ground, the engine fires. It allows the rocket to land softly in an upright position.

Space tourism companies test their rockets. During each test flight, they monitor the spacecraft to see how it handles space travel. They see how different temperatures and forces affect the spacecraft. They also test how the flights might affect passengers.

SpaceX's Falcon 9 rocket takes off during a test flight.

Some tests have failed, and the spacecrafts have crashed. In 2014, Virgin Galactic's spacecraft crashed during a test over the Mojave Desert. One pilot died in the crash. Other tests have been perfect. Virgin Galactic, SpaceX, and Blue Origin have had many successful tests. None of the companies want to send people into space until they are sure their flights will be safe.

This Virgin Galactic test flight in 2018 was a success.

The New Spaceships

Blue Origin is developing the New Shepard spacecraft. Six tourists will be able to board a small capsule on top of a rocket. The rocket will launch and carry the capsule high in the air. No pilot or crew will be on board. Instead, computers will fly the ship. The rocket will drop off as the capsule goes up to the Karman line. The passengers will then experience four minutes of weightlessness, while viewing Earth from space.

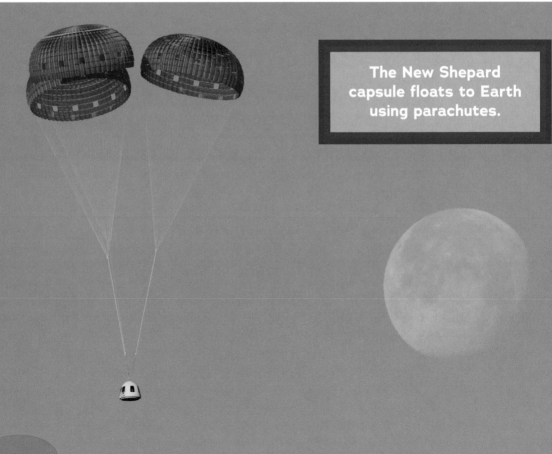

The New Shepard capsule floats to Earth using parachutes.

Virgin Galactic is testing its new spaceship too. First, its plane, WhiteKnightTwo, takes off from a runway. Then it drops SpaceShipTwo from its central wing when it is 50,000 feet (15,240 m) above Earth. SpaceShipTwo then launches its rockets and speeds toward space. At the right moment, it will cut its engines. Passengers will be at the edge of space. They'll feel weightless there. They will also see Earth's curving surface. Then gravity will pull the spaceship down. The pilot will land SpaceShipTwo back on Earth.

SpaceX has a big goal for its first space tourism flight. Its spacecraft is called Starship. Tourists will travel around the moon in the spaceship. It will carry up to one hundred passengers. The first passenger has already paid for his trip. He is the Japanese businessman Yusaku Maezawa. The spacecraft will orbit close to the moon's surface. Passengers will even see Earth rise over the moon! The entire trip will take about six days.

SpaceX's first tourists will visit the moon and see Earth rising over it.

STARSHIP IS SPACEX'S SPACECRAFT MEANT FOR TOURISTS.

▼

Once in space, the spaceship will deploy solar panels. The panels will collect energy from the sun and turn it into electricity. This will help power the spacecraft. SpaceX plans to launch its first passenger trip in 2023.

Space Fact or Fiction

Space tourists can take a balloon to space. That's fiction. But balloons may soon take tourists to the edge of space! Both World View and Zero 2 Infinity have space tourism balloons. Their trips will allow tourists to have some of the experiences of space. The helium balloons will lift passengers in a capsule. They'll go to the top of Earth's atmosphere. Passengers will see Earth curving beneath the blackness of space. World View will charge $75,000 for a ticket.

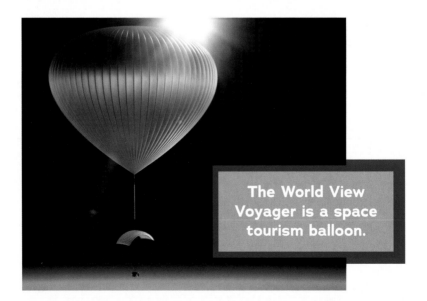

The World View Voyager is a space tourism balloon.

Chapter 3

TRAINING FOR SPACE

Traveling to space is risky. So space tourists need to train for their trip. They need to learn how to move around in low gravity. They also need to learn how to deal with fast acceleration. The forces from fast acceleration are very strong. These are called g-forces. They can be hard on a person's body. Space tourists need to be in good shape to travel into space. They also need to know how to operate the spacecraft in case of an emergency.

When a rocket launches into space, the astronauts on board experience incredible g-forces.

A space tourist trains in the Yuri A. Gagarin Cosmonaut Training Center.

The first space tourists traveled in Russian spacecraft. They trained in Russia at the Yuri A. Gagarin Cosmonaut Training Center. They spent eight months training. They practiced flying the spacecraft using video simulations. They learned how to fix the spacecraft too. They also worked out in a gym. Space tourism companies will have their own types of training. Each tourist will need to prepare for space.

Feeling G-forces

All space training also includes using a centrifuge. This is a machine that tests how people handle g-forces. G-forces can make it hard to breathe. Blood takes longer to reach the brain. This can make people pass out. A centrifuge quickly whips people around in a circle. Space tourists can see how their bodies will handle g-forces. They can also practice ways to deal with the forces.

A centrifuge helps prepare people for the strong g-forces of space travel.

Training in a Jet

Space tourists can also train by flying in a special airplane. The plane flies high above Earth. It then arcs and quickly dives down. This is called a parabolic arc. This flight pattern makes people feel weightless for about twenty-five seconds. Tourists will feel what it is like in zero gravity.

Space tourists learn what it feels like to be weightless before traveling to space.

Chapter 4

FUTURE SPACE TOURISM

Rockets and spacecraft may not be the only ways that tourists will visit space. They may also go there on an elevator. This elevator could be 22,000 miles (35,406 km) high. Japan and China are working on space elevators. China predicts its space elevator will be built by 2045. Japan thinks its elevator will be done in 2050.

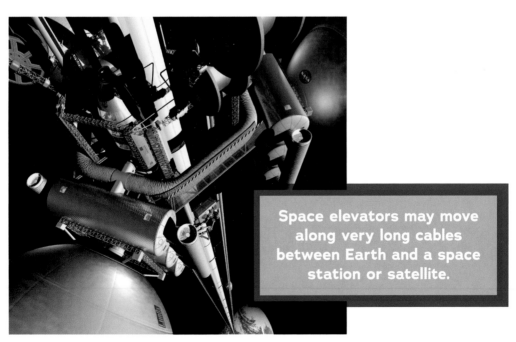

Space elevators may move along very long cables between Earth and a space station or satellite.

This illustration shows a space elevator on the surface of the moon.

A space elevator will have one incredibly long cable. One end of the cable will be attached to Earth. The other end will be attached to a large asteroid or space station. As Earth spins, it will swing the cable, holding the space elevator upright. Vehicles will be able to move along the cable. They will bring passengers into space. Scientists on the ISS are testing this idea using two small satellites connected by a steel cable.

A Luxury Space Hotel

After getting into space, tourists may have a beautiful place to stay too. Orion Span plans to build a luxury hotel in space. Its space hotel will be called Aurora Station. It will orbit Earth. Up to four guests will be able to stay there in two bedrooms. The first guests may arrive in 2022.

Tourists may one day spend a vacation in a space hotel, such as Aurora Station.

Guests will sleep in a room like this on Aurora Station.

Orion Span

A stay at the hotel is expensive though. It will cost $9.5 million for twelve days. Guests will orbit Earth every ninety minutes. That means they will see over one hundred sunrises and sunsets during their stay!

A Vacation on Mars?

What if tourists want to stay longer in space? They may be able to visit Mars. SpaceX wants to build a large city on Mars. It plans to start a colony there as early as 2028. People could then visit the planet, but it would be a long vacation. The trip to reach Mars from Earth would take many months.

A Mars colony may be built inside a dome on the planet's surface.

Space tourism is new. It is something only a few very wealthy people have experienced. As more companies build spacecraft, more people will be able to visit space. They'll see beyond Earth's atmosphere and fly to the moon. Maybe someday they'll even take vacations on other planets!

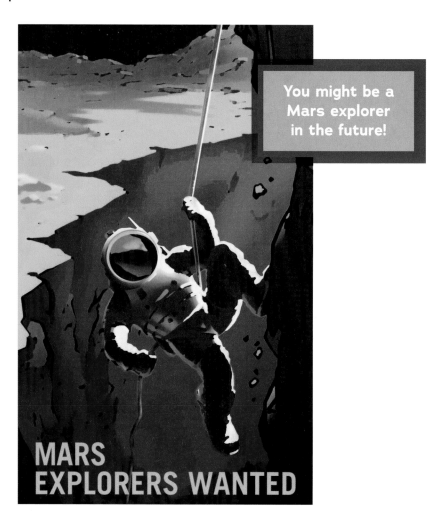

You might be a Mars explorer in the future!

MARS EXPLORERS WANTED

3D Printer Activity

NASA hopes to land astronauts on Mars in the 2030s to prepare the way for tourists. No humans have visited Mars yet, but NASA has landed rover missions on the planet. One of those rovers is *Curiosity*. Use the link below to make a model of the *Curiosity* rover with a 3D printer.

PAGE
PLUS
http://qrs.lernerbooks.com/dwev

Glossary

acceleration: the rate that something speeds up

astronaut: a person who is trained to travel on a space mission

atmosphere: the gases that surround a planet

engineer: a person whose job is to take knowledge of science and materials and think of better ways to design machines and other structures

g-force: force created by fast acceleration

gravity: a force that pulls things toward very large objects such as planets and stars; the bigger the object, the stronger the pull of gravity

Karman line: the name for the imaginary boundary that marks the beginning of space, which is about 62 miles (100 km) above sea level

rocket: a part of a spacecraft used to launch it from the surface of Earth

rover: a vehicle used for exploring and investigating another planet or object in space

weightless: not feeling the pull of gravity

Learn More about Space Tourism

Books

Gitlin, Marty. *Careers in Personal Space Travel*. Ann Arbor, MI: Cherry Lake, 2019. You may be able to work in space tourism one day! Find out how in this book.

Goldstein, Margaret J. *Private Space Travel: A Space Discovery Guide*. Minneapolis: Lerner Publications, 2017. Learn more about what space tourism trips will be like.

Wood, John. *Space Technology: Landers, Space Tourism, and More*. New York: Gareth Stevens, 2019. Discover all kinds of space technology in this book, including space tourism technology.

Websites

4 Fun Facts about Space Travel
https://www.cbc.ca/kidscbc2/the-feed/4-fun-facts-about-space-travel
Explore some fun facts about space travel and space tourism.

NASA Kids' Club
https://www.nasa.gov/kidsclub/index.html
You can learn many things about space and space travel on this NASA site.

Our Universe for Kids—Famous Space Explorers
https://www.ouruniverseforkids.com/famous-people-involved-space
-exploration/
Learn about some of the explorers who paved the way for space tourists.

Index

Photo Acknowledgments

Image credits: Cover: SpaceX. Text: NASA, pp. 4, 5, 16; NASA/Bill White, p. 6; NASA/Joel Kowsky, p. 7; Blue Origin, pp. 8, 10, 14; Studio23/Shutterstock.com, p. 9; SpaceX, pp. 11, 12, 17, 19; Gene Blevins/AFP/Getty Images, p. 13; Fredric J Brown/AFP/Getty Images, p. 15; World View Enterprises, Inc., p. 18; Epsilon/Getty Images, p. 20; GCTC via ESA, p. 21; Maxim Marmur/AFP/Getty Images, p. 22; NASA/Pat Rawlings, p. 23; Walter Myers/Stocktrek Images/Getty Images, p. 24; Orion Span, Inc., pp. 25, 26; Steven Hobbs/Stocktrek Images/Getty Images, p. 27; NASA/KSC, p. 28; NASA/JPL-Caltech, p. 29.

3d print activity on p. 29: NASA/JPL.